Love Deep

'Love Deep'

A poetic voyage through love's many meandering cycles, its endless yearnings, and the overlapping, in-the-meantime moments that define our lives.

Karen Lugay

Love Deep/Karen Lugay

ISBN: 978-0-6151-6310-9

Printed in the United States of America.

Cover Design by Karen Lugay

Book images courtesy of the wonderfully talented photographers at Stockxchng.

I dedicate this book to my one and only sister and sibling and my mom for all their support, and to all those who have been part of my life experiences past and present. Finally I dedicate the pages of this book to all who will read through them. I hope you find value in what is presented.

Table Of Contents

In My Words--------13

What Eyes See--------15

My Element--------17

What Tickles The Soul--------19

Invisible--------21

What The Day Doesn't Know--------25

Guarded Gates--------26

Distance--------29

With You--------33

Into Your Heart's Chamber--------36

The Crown She Wears--------38

The Silence--------40

Someone Else--------42

Tears--------44

I Woke--------45

Vacuum--------47

Love's Deceit--------48

As If For The First Time--------53

I Wait--------54

Your Patience--------56

Let's Always Be Honest--------58

Love Undefined--------60

Smitten--------65

Long Term Relationship--------66

Longing--------67

Bleeding Hearts--------68

Resolve Is--------69

಼

Before Intimate Love
There is the Self ...

IN MY WORDS

In my words
The emblem of my soul is found.
In my words
I am fully awake
And boundless.

In my words
The wholeness of me is imprinted
And the language of truth speaks out loud.
My welcomed buffer amid life's fallacies,
My emblem of certainty amongst confusion.

In my words
I escape the jagged edges of the world
To slide along my soul's cushion
Towards redemption.

In my words
I share with you
My authentic self
Unrestrained,
Free as a bird in flight.

In my words
My light emanates
Through these pages.
In my words
I feel you and you feel me.

WHAT EYES SEE

You watch me
But do you see me?
In your laser sharp scrutiny
Do you look beyond the shell
That veils the inner parts of me?

From a distance our eyes meet,
Images of me your eyes formulate.
As anticipation germinates,
A cacophony of thoughts ensues.

Anticipation reverts to excitement
As your perception of me waivers.
Am I truly what you see?
You wonder

Could the parts of me
In their summation
Welcome your intrusion?
You wonder

Our distance hides too much.
From up close will your mind
Find truth and depth to its visions of me?
You wonder

As we move nearer
From scrutiny evolves greater inquiry
As your mind screams
To speak out loud
Its silent monologue.

You wonder
Is she the illusion or the reality?

MY ELEMENT

I'm in my own element now.
Do you not see the gaze in my eyes?
Under their thick film of non-transparency
The gateways are locked.
The door to my soul
Is impenetrable now,
So don't force it.
Exist for me only in silence.
Keep your thoughts still
Until I need them awaken.

Today I can't be me.
In this moment I share with myself,
I don't see you.
So let me be
For now at least
In my own element.

Why do you look at me that way?
Don't harbor such worry.
I know my retreat
Leads you to query.
For that I'm truly sorry,
But for now I am in
My own median.

I'm painting on my own canvas.
For now I form the strokes that define me.
Enter now as an intruder,
A foreign presence
Within my element.

Understand the value of your absence now,
Appreciate the significance of your patience with me now,
Realize the importance of you still being here
Even in your confusion.

And know that once this has passed
My regenerated soul will welcome you to its bosom.
My body will share with you
The rejuvenation gained in that one moment
When you laid await
And allowed it to be
In its own element.

WHAT TICKLES THE SOUL

What tickles the soul
Brings to full view
The person within.

What tickles the soul
Jolts the heart
And awakens life's wonders
As longing eyes welcome
Each new discovery,
And life's possibilities are brought
Back into existence.

In those moments
Unfulfilled dreams find a nest of hope
From which to germinate.

What tickles the soul
Makes all the world well again.
Old conflicts find resolution
And the song of the soul resonates,
Its joy made visible,
Its bliss undeniable.

For this joy and bliss
Amplifies its melody
And reveals its majesty.
And so it cries out
All is well
All is well in me
And all is well with the world!

INVISIBLE

The quiet one
Invisible,
Dressed in a cloak of silence.
Adorned in an observable shyness,
Others she leads to retreat,
Their minds made anxious by her quiescence.

The quiet one
Invisibility and solitude
Are her foreboding traits.
Her presence barely moves the air around her,
Her ambiguity barely merits interest.

The quiet one
Unseen and misunderstood
Shrinks into her ball of isolation.
In her withdrawal
The wonders held within her stillness become hidden.

But dear quiet one I tell you
If only you knew
That it's the soul's eye which
Stares at your beauty
And knows you well.

And from its vantage point
You are as visible as a sunny day.

ℭß

Unreachable

WHAT THE DAY DOESN'T KNOW

What the day doesn't know
The night discloses.
Unveiled is all that is entailed
In the innermost trails
Of the cavity of the mind.

What the day doesn't know
The night entertains.
Unfulfilled desires maintained,
In dreams they find escape
By morning's rising
The curtains raised
And all is revealed.

What the day doesn't know
The night examines.
New arenas entered,
Adventures rendered mellifluously.
Abstract plots surface superfluously
From a place unknown, yet majestic.

In the night's quietude
The mind weaves its way
Through the entangled web
And complexities that define it.

GUARDED GATES

Blindly you trample through
That which surrounds
Your silhouette of emptiness.
No definition or route you pursue.
Drowning in the blur of your musty path
You try to make your way;
Fumbling through the haze
Searching for the familiarity you seek.

So much to prove, so little unveiled.
The weight of your ego
Dominates your senses,
It dulls your spark,
And rapes you of your genuineness.
Yet you welcome its invasion
As it tears through
The armor of your skin.

And for what?
To say that you're the man?
That you run the show?
What honor is there in that?

Total retreat all in the name of saving yourself.
True freedom
Lost in a mesh
Of unyielding pride.

You *are* a person enclosed,
A canopy of fallacies,
Steel walls set against the world.
For you a little revealed is too much given,
And too much given
Is risking plenty.
Secrecy and mystery embellish
Within the framework of your emotions.

In everyway you want everything
But your heart strays from giving back
That which you seek.
In every way you seek everything
But your body fails to reciprocate.
In everyway you strive
For the spotlight.
You play the part,
Today you control the illusion.

At all costs you maintain the character
Fighting off eyes that dare to enter
Through your guarded gates.

Unshielded eyes that navigate
Deep into places
You struggle to keep hidden.
Will they pass your silhouette
Delving into the core of you?
If they seek to know the you
Under the mask
Will you fearlessly face their piercing gaze?

They see the image,
They witness the masquerade.
They know that there is
No joy in either.
They recognize that
You've made the truth
An abstraction;
A jagged plane
That to be accessed
Must be conquered.
Yet you remain lost in the debris of the illusion
Crouched behind the pillars of your fortress.

DISTANCE

If I were you
I'd ask why I care,
Why can't I adhere
To the reality that's there?
I'm here
And you're over there.

If I were you
I'd tell me that love is a past
That may have never been steadfast.
Holding on may be a task
If I try to mask
The reality that exists.
After all I'm here
And you're over there.

But didn't I say
That I was going to
Let go right away?
Set my life
Back to its old motion
As soon as I crossed the ocean?

Do you think my heart sees through the pretense?

'Cause it seems to be struggling

In its own war.

Pondering

Wondering

Desiring more and more of you.

Maybe in the present

We might be friends

And in the future

Perhaps make amends

For love coming

Too soon to an end.

Meandering Moments in Love

WITH YOU

Sitting with you
Life has no pace.
In the stillness of the night
Time passes.
Our bodies in sync,
Our minds adrift
As the streetlights
Carousel our faces.

Your eyes pierce through me;
I travel deep within them.
They take me to a new place
Embodied with pleasure,
Where no boundaries are met.

Here I wanna stay
Laced in your embrace.
No queries, no squabbles
No fuss, no fight.

An ocean of pleasures
Pulsating.
The darkness camouflaging
Our explorations,
Here there are no limitations.

My impassioned mind wants more,
But at last the night must end.
You leave.
My hopes of unending euphoria quailed
In that final moment,
That final kiss,
That final goodbye.

The invisible imprints
Of your slender fingers linger still,
Tell-tale signs
Of our nighttime rendezvous.

It seems too cruel.
Just enough of you to feed the fire
Yet not enough at all.
In my dreams
I fill in the blank moments yet to be.
In the morning
A new day of possibilities,
The physical remnants
Of yesterday's pleasures
Washed away as I shower.

My body anew,
My mind relaxed,
My heart wanting replenishment.
They don't forget,
Hour by hour
They long once again
For the familiarity
Of your presence.

INTO YOUR HEART'S CHAMBER

Let me enter
Into your heart's chamber,
That place where things seem clear
And life goes beyond existence.

Let me enter
Here in your heart's chamber,
Let it permeate me
Envelope the framework of me
Consuming all that is me.

Let me enter
Within your heart's chamber.
To explore what is there,
To make discoveries,
To envision all the possibilities
Ensued from your heart's pervasive melodies
That sing to me
Holding me steadily within their dominion.

Let me enter
Locked in your heart's chamber,
Let me stay there
If only for a moment

To wonder, to wander
Deep inside
This love rendered timeless.

Oh how sublime
The web you've spun
Has become mine,
Yet happily in this
Lover's maze I navigate.
Under your gaze
I migrate steadily
Into your heart's chamber.

THE CROWN SHE WEARS

The crown she wears
Probed high
Nestled well within its resting place,
Vestige of the royalty
Sure to have been.

The crown she wears
Invisible to undiscerning eyes,
But glaring to *these* eyes
Absorbed by the magnificence of her,
Awed by the presence of her.

They remain unblinking,
Teary and dazed eyes,
Gawking stares,
Trapped within her formidable web.
Impervious to all competing fixations
Within her periphery,
Her imaginary "QueenDom".

The crown she wears
Adorns her,
But doesn't define her.
Conforms to the queen
But sabotages not her humility.

Indeed her person stays intact
"Hot headedness" is unbecoming the queen.

The crown she wears
Has made its place.
An endearing presentation of her sovereignty,
But never will it consume her.
Quietly it plays it role,
But all graced with the queen can't miss it.

The crown she wears
Puts all the people to notice,
'Cause the crown they see
Comes from what she gives wholesomely
A reflection of her goodness in its entirety.
For the crown she wears
Is in her admirable qualities.

THE SILENCE

Within the silence
In the moment when our eyes first meet
Across the room,
One step in front the other leads you slowly to me.
Between that silence,
With hearts anticipating
We make an agreement.
From then on
Mutual understanding and discovery
We hope to cultivate.

Within the silence
In the moment of knowing each other;
Between the space of the long conversations
We never want to end,
We feel the "rightness" of this thing we've got going
Growing stronger with each minute spent together.

Within that silence
Our connection is eminent.

Within the silence
Between the space of our lovemaking
As heightened pleasures slowly dissipate,
We contemplate
How comfortably we fit into
This love that we have nurtured.

Within the silence
We know that this one is for forever.

SOMEONE ELSE

You belong to someone else.
I was just passing through.
A chance encounter.
Who knew
That love would brew
Anew
Amongst these crude circumstances?

You belong to someone else.
At first her existence unknown,
So I proceeded
Extracting the love I needed
As I yielded to your affections unheeded.
You belong to someone else.
I was just a stranger passing through,
Unsuspecting
Expecting the truth in your eyes
Hoping they won't telling lies.

Now I stand alone.
If only I had been told
Before events unfolded,
Before feelings were consummated,
Before I was consumed,
By emotions unabated.

You belong to someone else.
I wish I had known
Before hearts became molded,
Folded into a fire of desire
Only to be smoldered
By the ashes of forbidden love.

TEARS

Tears cascade
Amid silent screams,
'Could have beens',
Which have become her torment.
Once again in a sad place
Too many times revisited.
Too many impassioned encounters
Ending prematurely.

Lost potential,
Promises never verbalized,
Yet lust's momentum was energized
Fed by a perforation of desire,
Infatuation,
Insatiable enthusiasm
Unyielding to reality's knock;
Its warning stubborn minds mocked.

Young hearts succumbed
To a love never actualized;
Strangers beckoned to each other's wonder
Playing host to each other's longing.
The idea of love was entertained,
But in the end none was witness to it.
In the end only tears remain.

I WOKE

This morning I woke
Tear filled eyes
Dreams riddled with fear and longing;
Yearning belonging, needing prolonging
The image of you in my subconscious adjoining.

There you were
On the floor, your body entwined with mine.
An older you, somehow new to me
But familiar still.
The same feeling you ensued in me
Even in my dreams.

In my night's chronicle
Each moving particle
A conglomeration of a whole
Seemingly real to me, not perceived.
In my dreams the idea of you conceived,
The language of love retrieved
Bellowed from a heart
Bearing no immunity to you.

My body knows you too well.
In my night's chronicle
It renders to your emblem,
The realm of you I surrender to.

VACUUM

Loneliness is a funny thing.
It puts you on the brink.
It brings you to scary places,
A vesicle of confusion
Pulling you further from yourself.
A deluge of unhappiness
Pushing you towards hopelessness.
The chokehold of uncertainty and doubt
Tossing you into an empty space.

You try to get out;
Claws edged into the
Walls of its prison.
At a distance
The blur of escape cajoles you further in.

Eyes swell up
As desperation lurks.
Unhappiness, Frustration
They find a breeding ground
Feet cemented in agony's domain
A house of pain
Feasts on your emotions.

LOVE'S DECEIT

In the storm of my emotions
Insanity looms,
Yet my loneliness moves me closer to him,
If only he cared.
The one who could have been
If only he cared.
The granter of pleasure
If only he cared.

My loneliness suctions my soul
Into a sullenness
That overwhelms me.
My need I can't explain.
Love beckons,
But it plays tricks on me.
It hides away where
I cannot see.

It deceives me
Makes me believe in its feasibility.
It coaxes me into trying harder.
My desperate heart awaits its entrance,
But love taunts me.
It stays hidden.

It has me pumped up now.

Its deceit fuels my search even more.

I want it even more.

I would sacrifice even more.

Pride and self-worth

Go to the wind.

Like a virgin seduced

I've yielded to it.

Gladly I give in

If only love would

Make its appearance.

I yearn to see its face

My crazed desire pushes me

Deeper and deeper into its maze.

The Real Thing

AS IF FOR THE FIRST TIME

I love how at each encounter
It's as if it's the first time we're seeing each other.
How you joyously recount the images of me you hold in my absence.
Even when I'm simply laying next to you
You seem to savor every inch of me.
Even when I think you've had your fill of me
You always want more.

Thank you for loving me wholeheartedly,
Thank you for loving me unconditionally,
Thank you for loving the rough exterior of my personality,
Thank you for loving me in the moments when I retreat into myself
And in the aftermath, loving me as if those not so good moments never happened.
Thank you for loving me everyday
As if you were seeing me for the first time.

I WAIT

Why do I wait you ask?
I know you expect to hear the...
"I want it to be special,
The perfect moment" talk
The "I wanna wait 'til I get married" talk
"I wanna wear white on my wedding day" talk or the
"I wanna stay pure for that one and only someone"

Sorry to disappoint
For my reasons don't mirror these.
None make my list.
I wait not because I feel the grandeur of the moment magnified by the sacrifice,
The unsuspecting virgin I'm not.
I look not to get attached to my first victim as is often the myth,
Not the 'never been touched type'.
True the cherry waits to be popped,
But dormant it is not.

I say I have too much self-restraint.
Naked before a wanting man I've stood
Yet I wait
Throbbing with desire I've been
Yet I wait
Wanting and needing I've been
Yet I wait

A ready body prepared for a man's entry,
Breasts ripe with anticipation
Yet I wait.

No I'm not a tease, far from it.
None was without knowledge of my desires and limits
Yet willing participants they remained.
Perhaps the thrill of messing with the nice girl virgin
Or the prospects of being the "one" to break through.

But the right time with the right person,
After it's all said and done it has to be more than just a good fuck.
That, I know many a man have had with me in their dreams
And to me that's not enough.

So many opportunities passed,
Some never realized.
Those obstacles in the way
Were perhaps for the best in the end.

Why do I wait?
I wait because I know that when it happens it happens,
And regardless of how it turns out
It will happen as it was meant to be
And all of me will give into it completely.

YOUR PATIENCE

You pursued me earnestly
With grace you etched your way into my world
Never at first announcing your intentions
But always giving to me selflessly
As you patiently awaited the day
Until I figured out that
I wanted you as much as you wanted me

ॐ

You touched me with care
Easing gracefully into me.
I open up slowly
Like petals welcoming the morning's sun.

This moment so many times we have envisioned;
I wonder whether your patience will hold
Now in these awkward initial
Strokes of our lovemaking.

You see my face tense as you slide slowly
Into my velvet chamber
As it willingly succumbs to your advancing.
Unhurriedly you allow the momentum to build
Our rhythm becoming symmetric to our heartbeat.
Amid the sounds of our climax
We feel the river of our longing flow through us
Dressing us with the aftermath
Of the night's escapade.

LET'S ALWAYS BE HONEST

I always want us to be
Honest with each other,
To let ourselves be
Whoever we are in the moment
And share the things about ourselves
We may think we need to hide.

When I met you
I knew that I had met someone
Who knew me from within.
From that first encounter we blossomed
At first as friends with mutual respect for the other
And from that mutual friendship
A deeper understanding evolved,
Then feelings of affection
And finally love.

And because I love you
I want us to always be honest with each other
'Cause you are my best friend and my closest ally.

So let's stay steadfast to our commitment
To being unshielded in the presence of each other
To always let our true, uninhibited self shine through.

Remember that regardless
Of how seemingly overwhelming your feelings and emotions,
I'm willing to act as the buffer
So that you can relinquish
Some of what ails you from within.

Know that I am there for you,
That I love you,
And that I will always be honest with you.

LOVE UNDEFINED

I tell myself
I am not exactly sure what we are yet
Although I know that being with you
Makes my heart soar.

I experience it every time
Our eyes lock in an inferno of passion,
Every time our hands are webbed together,
And every time our heads are side by side
As we lay in quiet solitude
Taking in the feelings of love
Bearing themselves in that silent moment.

Every time I look at you
I know I am loving you more and more.
With each day that elapses between
The times we see each other
Slowly my love is made stronger.

But still I know I am holding back.
Although I am certain that
There's no denying your love for me,
I admit I'm afraid.

If I love you just as much
As you love me
Would that equilibrium be the end of us?
You're so used to being
The man who's waiting for me to love him
And in the meantime loves me anyway, and despite its oddness
That has been the silent agreement between us.

So I remain content in not exactly being sure
Of what we are yet,
But what I'm really saying is
That I'm scared like crazy to tell you that I love you
Because in the moment I do
No longer will I be the
The girl you're waiting to say "I love you".

So I let my love for you remain undefined
Because I'm uncertain whether
After those words are spoken
You will still love me the same.

But truly I want to gaze into your eyes
And scream out
"I love you sweetie!"
Because I do,
I do love you.

So let my love be now defined
Because I want to be free to love you
The way you love me.

Long-Term Relationship

SMITTEN

Know that I appreciate all that you are.
As the days of our relationship multiply
Know that I'm still smitten by you.

My mind still cultivates
Thoughts of you when you are not there.
My body seeks only to meander its way
There amongst the contours of your haven
To find its place within the spaces therein.

Know that my heart yearns to more greatly
Know you with each day that passes.
Know that I love you

LONG-TERM RELATIONSHIP

Honey I admit that I wonder how our love will survive the uneventful days
When we spend more and more still moments together
When it's not always a weekend trip here, dinner or a movie there
When kids and pets and family outings come into the picture

As we get settled into this relationship
I know that because we love each other
Our days doing nothing but holding
And sharing each other in silence
Will keep the vigor going
Because each other is all the excitement that we need

ॐ

I need to be all that you need
That which allows the joy in you to ascend
That which multiplies the fulfillment in you
That which brings the love in you to higher highs
That which leads all that is in you to know how much I love you

LONGING

I feel you honey
I feel you
Do you know what that means?
It means that even in your absence
Images of you wrap my mind.

And this never ending desire commands
The deepest parts of me
And calls my heart to hold you near.

క

The week's end I await
Only for the treasure of your company.

The week's end I await
Only to cancel out the space between our times spent together,
Only to forget for a moment
The oceans between us,
The distance in this long-distance relationship.

The week's end I await
Only to show you how much I cherish you.

BLEEDING HEARTS

How did things turn out this way?
I never knew what forever felt like...
Until today.
After the careless words uttered
It would seem that nothing more can be said
To make things right again.

How do I convince you that
I carry the pain I've caused you
More heavily than you could imagine?

How do I convince you that
That my whole being pleads for your forgiveness,
And begs that you understand
How truly sorry I am?

RESOLVE IS

Resolve is
Freeing a caged mind,
Bursting the seams of a welded heart,
Releasing a breath held in too long,
Prying open eyes shut
Into blindness.

Resolve is
Words held in silence
Amplified,
Streaming through ears
Ready to receive them.

Resolve is
The welcome surprise of a random smile.
Rest to the soul,
A long awaited sleep.
The cocoon of redundancy unraveled,
And in its place
The sprouting of much needed newness.
The end and the beginning.

Resolve is clarity,
A guided path,
A letting go,
The forward button to the next experience,
Life no longer in reverse.

CB

"There is only one happiness in life, to love and be loved".

~George Sand

"To love and be loved is to feel the sun from both sides".

~David Viscott

"The love we give away is the only one we keep".

~Elbert Hubbard

ᥫ

"Nothing contributes so much to tranquilize the mind as a steady purpose-A point on which the soul may fix its intellectual eye".

~Mary Wollstonecraft
Shelly

About The Author

KAREN LUGAY is a young professional residing in New York City where she is currently a Registered Dietitian. Amid her passion for food and other interests, is her need to write about the deepest aspects of life and love. Thus has emerged her desire to create this her first book of poetry. Karen writes openly from the heart, expressing the abstractions of her own life experiences as well as those of others.

www.ingramcontent.com/pod-product-compliance
Lightning Source LLC
Chambersburg PA
CBHW032027040426
42448CB00006B/756